GUARANTEED PROFITS WITH SMALL STOCKS

ALSO BY R. MAX BOWSER

BOOKS

Making Dollars With Pennies: How the Small Investor Can Beat the Wizards on Wall Street

Penny Stock Winners: True Stories of Successful Investors

Warrants: The Speculator's Friend

EDITOR, MONTHLY NEWSLETTERS

The Bowser Report

The Bowser Directory of Small Stocks

GUARANTEED PROFITS WITH SMALL STOCKS

> THE ONLY STOCK MARKET INVESTMENT SYSTEM THAT COMES WITH A $5,000 GUARANTEE

R. Max Bowser

MARATHON INTERNATIONAL BOOK COMPANY

Madison, Indiana

> The author, R. Max Bowser, is offering the $5,000 based on following his game plan as described in this book. The publisher is not offering this guarantee. Any correspondence regarding the guarantee should be sent to R. Max Bowser, c/o *The Bowser Report*, P.O. Box 6278, Newport News, VA 23606.

MARATHON INTERNATIONAL BOOK COMPANY
PO Box 40
Madison, IN 47250-0040 U.S.A.
Telephone (812) 273-4672
Fax (812) 273-8964
E-mail: jwortham@seidata.com

Copyright © 2004 by R. Max Bowser

All rights reserved under the Pan-American and International Copyright Conventions. Except for the inclusion of brief quotations in a review, no part of this book may be reproduced or utilized in any form or by any means, electronic or mechanical, including photocopying, recording or by an information storage and retrieval system, without permission in writing from the publisher, Marathon International Book Company.

Library of Congress Cataloging-in-Publication Data

Bowser, R. Max.
  Guaranteed profits with small stocks: the only stock market investment system that comes with a $5,000 guarantee / R. Max Bowser.-- 1st ed.
    p. cm.
Includes index.
  ISBN 1-928877-02-8 (Hardcover)
  1. Penny stocks. 2. Speculation. I. Title.
HG6041.B688 2003
332.63'22--dc21
                                      2003012146

First Edition • First Printing
Printed on acid-free paper
Printed and bound in the United States of America

DEDICATION

To those who profitably subscribed to the Bowser Game Plan for over two decades.

PREFACE

WE HAVE SPENT OVER THREE DECADES PERFECTING OUR approach to stocks selling for $3 a share or less. This book presents our perfected version of the Bowser Game Plan, which has been battle tested.

In effect, this tome is the manual for successfully utilizing our monthly publication—*The Bowser Report*. In fact, all of the material that appears herein has been published at one time or other in the newsletter.

One of the key tools we use in eliminating undesirable companies from our universe is our Rating System, which is fully explained herein.

Finally, we've had a long-time relationship with many of our newsletter subscribers, who are brave souls in that they are dealing with equities that are scorned by many in the investment community.

As a consequence, we call the followers of the Bowser Game Plan—Buckaroos. . . . We salute these hardy folks wherever they are on this globe and dedicate this book to these Buckaroos!

> – R. Max Bowser
> 757/877-5979
> E-mail: ministocks@aol.com

FOREWORD

WHO DARES OFFER A $5,000 GUARANTEE IF YOU scrupulously follow his stock recommendations and his rules explicitly for buying and selling and then lose money. . . . Of course, it's Max Bowser.

As feisty editor of *The Bowser Report* and a monthly columnist for *The Moneypaper*, journalist turned minipriced stock preacher, Max has spent decades spreading the message small can be beautiful and big can be bad.

Over the years, he has perfected his approach to picking winners in the invisible $3-per-share market. And, all you need to get started is a $54 subscription to his newsletter, which caters to the little guy.

During the Internet stock madness when large-cap institutional P/Es went over 100—if the high-flying IPO had any earnings, Max Bowser warned the little investor about the absurd valuations. In return, Wall Street shunned his microcaps as too risky, even though many had much better relative intrinsic values than the issues the "Street" was touting.

Many fallen angels sell below $5 and ironically are in the penny-stock category, which the Street has scorned. . . . Institutional guidelines prevent security analysts from following these new penny issues, creating a vacuum. . . . Now the moment for Max Bowser and his value-packed mini-growth stocks has arrived.

Centering only on stock selling at $3 a share or under, *The Bowser Report*'s loyal Buckaroo readers learn to buy low, prune losers and harvest winners early. His Rating System has 12 criteria, out of which an 8 or higher is a buy, This helps focus on promising companies. Diversification prevents risking too much on any one stock in this speculative area.

These are sound ideas for a difficult niche.

– Robert J. Flaherty
Editor and Chairman
Equities Magazine

GUARANTEED PROFITS WITH SMALL STOCKS

TABLE OF CONTENTS

Penny Stocks Beat Blue Chips In Bear Market 15

The Buckaroo's Creed 19
This is the Bowser Game Plan in a nutshell

Proceeds From Sales 21
An important part of the Game Plan

Anatomy Of A Portfolio 25
A demonstration of how the Game Plan works

Individuals vs. Mutual Funds 29
We isolate the weak points in open-end mutual funds

Whom Would You Bet With? 35
A market gadfly and the potential of the individual

Start Your Own Mutual Fund 37
You don't have to be a financial wizard

Bowser Microcap Stock Index 41
A new way to measure performance of tiny companies

Lies! Lies! Lies! 47
The unethical prejudice against small corporations

Why They Don't Like Penny Stocks 55
It's the big boys versus the little guys

Joe Videmsek, Investor of the Year 57
Bowser stocks play a major role in Joe's retirement

You Need An Exit Strategy 67
The key to stock market survival

Buckaroo Memo: Wall Street Mantra 69
The establishment blind faith in high-priced stocks

Bowser Ratings 71
A quick overview of our Rating System

Our $5000 Guarantee 75
No one else has dared do this

Thoughts on Our $5,000 Guarantee 77
Why we think it's justified

Reaction to the $5,000 Guarantee 81
Some buckaroos respond

Bowserizing a Portfolio 85
The whole is greater than the bits and pieces

Frequently Asked Questions 91
We destroy some myths

The R. Max Bowser Saga 95

Comments From Those Who Have Used
     Max Bowser's Investment Strategies 97

The Humorous Side 101

Index 105

PENNY STOCKS BEAT BLUE CHIPS IN BEAR MARKET

Penny stocks are belittled by many in the financial community. However, if the same research techniques employed to identify successful higher-priced issues, are used to isolate the good penny stocks—then you can strike gold.

In this book, we identify those techniques.

In fact, we wondered how our little Bowser companies would do compared to some of the Blue Chips that make up the Dow Jones Industrial Average (DJIA). During a bear market.

We picked 12 we thought were representative of the DJIA (See Chart No. 1). How would they compete with the first 12 Companies of the Month, whose selection began at the beginning of the bear market? (Experts say the bear market started in Mar '00. Our study starts in Apr '00.)

The portfolio of 12 Bowser issues is a typical one, in that there were winners and losers. (Flour City, Magellan Pet and STRATESEC were busts.) And, once more we show that diversification is the investor's best friend (See Chart No. 2).

This comparison dramatically illustrates the leverage you have with our little ones. Also, it demonstrates how effectively your capital can be employed with penny stocks that represent profitable companies which have been carefully researched.

Theoretically, $1,000 was invested in each of the Dow stocks. Likewise, $1,000 was put into each new Company of the Month. And, the purchase price for each Bowser stock is the price the editor paid when he bought one week or later after all of our subscribers had a chance to buy.

The money in the Proceeds from Sales was generated by our Selling Plan and from sell recommendations made in the newsletter. (The Bowser gains would have been even greater if some of the Proceeds from Sales would have been used to buy succeeding Companies of the Month.)

CHART NO. 1
DOW JONES INDUSTRIAL COMPANIES

Stock	Price on 4-14-00 & Number Shares	Value 7-25-03	Dividends
Amer Express	$133.63/7.5	$342.00	$21.00
Citigroup	57.75/17.3	791.13	33.00
Coca Cola	46.78/21.4	963.86	45.00
DuPont	56.13/17.8	795.48	75.00
ExxonMobil	78.75/12.7	454.15	66.00
GenElectric	144.94/6.9	196.17	33.00
IBM	106.00/9.4	785.37	15.00
Merck	63.50/15.7	903.06	54.00
Proct/Gamble	62.75/15.9	1423.85	60.00
SBC Comm	42.75/23.4	550.84	81.00
United Tech	56.63/17.5	1323.70	42.00
WalMart	55.13/18.1	1017.04	12.00
	$12,000	$9,546.65	$537.00
Total:	$10,083.68	Down 16%	

CHART NO. 2
BOWSER COMPANIES OF THE MONTH

Date of Purchase	Stock	Price/Shares	Proceeds From Sales	Value 7/25/03
4-24-00	Sterns/Lehm	$3.00/333	$2,224	
5-26-00	Rag Shops	2.25/444	1,942	
6-19-00	Exporation Co	3.00/333	2,457	
7-24-00	Emerson Radio	.88/1,136	4,910	
8-21-00	Alpha Pro	1.25/800	1,925	
9-25-00	Poore Bros	2.81/356		1,776
11-23-00	Magellan Pet	1.16/862	619	
11-20-00	Reliv Int'l	1.75/571	2,158	
12-26-00	STRATESEC	1.81/552	220	
1-22-01	Flour City	2.63/380	30	
2-20-01	Int'l Remote	2.23/448		1,635
3-19-01	Creative Host	<u>1.75/571</u>	<u>　　　</u>	<u>1,079</u>
		$12,000	$16,485	$4,490

Total: $20,975 / Up 75% / Annualized Gain: 20%

THE BUCKAROO'S CREED

(1) GIVE OUR PLAN A CHANCE BY FOLLOWING IT rigorously. Dedicate a specific amount of capital to creating your minipriced portfolio.

(2) Minipriced stocks (sometimes called microcaps) have two attractions: leverage and the small amount of capital needed. It's easier for a $2 stock to double to $4 than a $50 stock to double to $100. With the $5,000 needed to buy 100 shares of a $50 stock, you can have a diversified microcap portfolio.

(3) Minipriced issues are risky because these small companies do not have the assets to withstand poor management decisions, ineffective acquisitions, changes in the marketplace for the firm's products or services, etc.

(4) Risk is managed through diversification. We suggest you have  12 to 18 different issues, selected from stocks listed on page 4 of *The Bowser Report*. Purchase an equal number of shares of each stock.

(5) If you cannot accept losses in these stocks, then you are not psychologically attuned to stock

market investing. (All stocks, regardless of price, have an element of risk and, hence, losses.)

(6) Use our Selling Plan. Sell half when the stock doubles from your purchase price. Dispose of the remainder when it drops 25% from its most recent high after doubling. Also, if a company's performance deteriorates and we say sell—sell.

(7) Occasionally, after using our Selling Plan, you may find the stock price goes higher. However, "losing" this money can be offset by the many times that you sell at a nice profit and then see the price of your stock begin to slide.

(8) Patience is your greatest asset in managing a portfolio of minipriced stocks. The *average* holding time for a stock in the Editor's personal portfolio has been slightly over 25 months.

(9) Record keeping is important. It allows you to know your progress at all times. Keeping track of the *Proceeds from Sales* is vital, regardless of whether the money comes from an issue sold for a gain or from a loss.

(10) This should be a challenging and fun experience. The Beginner's Portfolio in *The Bowser Report* follows The Buckaroo's Creed.

PROCEEDS FROM SALES

If you own more than one stock, you have a portfolio. How you manage that portfolio determines how well you do.

We have a revolutionary method of portfolio management. Not because of some esoteric device. Not because of a formula that a mathematician with a Ph.D. compiled.

Its simplicity will astound you. But, it shouldn't. We've been writing about it for some time. It plays an integral role in managing our Beginner's Portfolio.

What is this great development in stock market portfolio management? PROCEEDS FROM SALES. . . . Whenever you sell an issue—regardless of whether at a loss or a profit—put those funds in Proceeds from Sales.

But, most investors, when asked, "How are you doing?"— merely compute the value of the stocks currently held. If they exceed their cost, the portfolio is doing great. However, if it's less than the cost, there is a gloomy assessment.

Completely ignored is the money generated from the sale of stock in the portfolio—whether at a loss or a profit.

To demonstrate the important role that Proceeds from Sales plays in evaluating your portfolio, we selected an 18-month period from April 2000 to September 2001. We chose this period because during that time, we had stocks that doubled and some that had to be sold at a loss.

The 18 stocks are shown in the accompanying chart. . . . Each one was a Company of the Month and 200 shares were acquired of every issue.

And, to digress for a minute, once again this exercise demonstrates how little capital—comparatively—is needed to buy 18 of our recommendations. Less than the cost of 200 shares of a $35 issue.

The chart shows that $4,510 was accumulated through the sale of both profitable and unprofitable issues. And, with this money, we are just shy $2,000 of liquidating the original cost of the portfolio.

We still have 13 stocks in the portfolio. They had a value of $5,035 on June 21, 2002. Add that amount to $4,510 and you have a total of $9,545. This is $2,571 more than our cost. We have an annualized gain of 17%, assuming that no issues were bought to replace the ones sold.

In the chart, we show two columns for Proceeds from Sales. This was done to accommodate the revenue generated by the Bowser Selling Plan—sell half of your holdings when the stock doubles from your cost and sell the remainder when it drops 25% from its most recent high after doubling.

What are the objections to this revolutionary portfolio management technique? Basically, there are two. And, both highlight the frailty of human behavior.

"I don't have time." Our answer: Actually, the time involved is minimal. Just set up something similar to our chart. But, for the day-to-day value of the portfolio, log that on a separate form. Or, there are computer programs that will follow your stocks for you. With one keystroke each day, you can see how each issue is doing.

"I've never bothered." Our answer: You are only hurting yourself if you don't keep tabs on Proceeds from Sales. Just looking at the current value gives you a distorted image of your portfolio. Add in the Proceeds from Sales and you have a true picture.

A couple of months ago we had an interesting phone conversation with Stephen J. Palaszewski, a long-time *Bowser* subscriber.

Dr. Palaszewski said that from time to time he calculates the current value of his portfolio and it will be less than his cost. But, when he adds in Proceeds from Sales, the portfolio is in the black by a goodly measure.

We didn't include brokerage fees in our computations. But, they have become so low that they are of less importance. Consequently, if we had used a broker who charged $10 a transaction, that would have deducted $280 from the total, as there were 28 buys and sales.

Including the commissions would have increased the cost to $7,044. The Proceeds total would have been reduced to $4,410. The total would have been $9,445. Our gain would have been reduced to 34% from 37%.

A FULLY-DEVELOPED MINIPRICED PORTFOLIO

(1) Recommendations/Price	Cost	Proceeds from Sales		Value 6/21/02
4/00 Stearns & Lehman ($2.63)	$526		$1,472	Merged
5/00 Rag Shop ($2.00)	400	$450	450	Sold
6/00 Exploration Co. ($2.75)	550	640	622	Sold
7/00 Emerson Radio ($0.75)	150	200		$163
8/00 Alpha Pro ($1.31)	262			188
9/00 Poore Bros. ($2.56)	512			602
10/00 Magellan Pet ($1.22)	244			178
11/00 Reliv Int'l ($1.50)	300			576
12/00 Stratesec ($1.88)	376		80	Sold
1/01 Flour City ($1.88)	376	188	318	Sold
2/01 Int'l Remote ($1.74)	348			596
3/01 Creative Host ($2.00)	400			290
4/01 Stake Tech ($1.53)	306			596
5/01 Conolog Corp ($1.83)	366		90	Sold
6/01 Tofutti Brands ($2.10)	420			610
7/01 Collectors Univ ($1.90)	380			204
8/01 Biospecifics ($2.49)	498			464
9/01 Immucell ($2.25)	450			568
	$6,864	$1,478	$3,032	$5,035

(1) 200 shares purchased of each recommendation.

Total value of Portfolio: $4,510 (Proceeds from Sales) plus $5,035 (value 6/21/02) = $9,545.

ANATOMY OF A PORTFOLIO

THERE ARE THREE WAYS YOU CAN BUILD A PORTFOLIO OF minipriced stocks: (1) The one-shot method; (2) One-month-at-a-time; (3) The I-know-best approach.

The One-Shot Method

Since Jan '92 we have written a column for *The Moneypaper* newsletter, which is not a hotbed for speculative stocks. It specializes in promoting the advantages of dividend reinvesting.

With dividend reinvesting, you buy shares of a stock that pay a nice cash dividend. Then, each time the dividend is paid, you have the company use the dividend cash to buy more shares. Thus, you build up your stock position without having to further pay brokerage fees.

Vita Nelson, editor/publisher of *The Moneypaper*, is a pioneering expert on dividend reinvesting. Also, she is an open-minded person who realizes that there are other approaches to stock market investing. Consequently, not only does our column appear in her publication monthly, but also that of Michael Burke.

Mr. Burke is well known for determining the future of the market by analyzing the sentiments of newsletter editors. He also writes about—primarily—big name stocks. In addition, he is editor of the highly-respected *Investors Intelligence* (914/632-0422).

The Moneypaper portfolio is a "one-shot" operation because in the first year (1992) we allocated $14,000 and used those theoretical funds to purchase 14 different stocks—buying $1,000 worth of each one.

We were very astute or very lucky that first year. During those first 12 months, we were up 54%. The $14,000 grew into $21,529.33 in one year.

As you can see in the accompanying chart, the portfolio has grown to its current size. No additional funds have been used. Just the original $14,000. . . . Here are lessons we learned while managing *The Moneypaper* portfolio:

(1) Most of the time the current value of the stocks is less than the original cost of $14,000. The 9/20/02 portfolio that we show has a value just a little bit above $14,000.

(2) THIS IS MOST IMPORTANT: The proceeds from previous sales is an integral part of the portfolio. Many ignore the funds generated by previous sales. They just concentrate on the

current value and if that figure is less than their cost—a feeling of despondency prevails.

(3) This theoretical portfolio is self-financing in that we have not added to the original $14,000. For example, when we bought Leading Brands, we took $1,000 from the proceeds-from-sales fund. This fund is now $42,464.51.

(4) Patience. This is a long-term proposition. There have been some months when the total value was less than the previous month.

The Moneypaper Portfolio

STOCK	Orig $	Shares*	(Date)	Price 9/20/02
American Medical Alert (NASDAQ:AMAC)	2.88	348	(8/96)	2.02
Millbrook Press (NASDAQ:MILB)	2.25	444	(12/98)	1.71
Reconditioned Systems (NASDAQ:RESY)	2.75	382	(5/99)	2.10
Alpha Pro Tech Ltd. (AMEX:APT)	1.31	764	(8/00)	0.84
Reliv International (NASDAQ:RELV)	1.13	443	(11/00)	5.00
Int'l Remote Imaging (AMEX:IRI).	1.74	574	(2/01)	2.01
Creative Host Services (NASDAQ:CHST)	1.00	100	(4/01)	1.81
BioSpecifics Tech (NASDAQ:BSTC).	2.49	402	(8/01)	1.05
Dynatronics Corp. (NASDAQ:DYNT)	1.00	100	(9/01)	0.71
Valley Forge Scientific (NASDAQ:VLFG)	2.35	426	(11/01)	1.85
Leather Factory, The (NASDAQ:TLF)	1.75	363	(3/02)	2.85
Nyer Medical Group (NASDAQ:NYER)	2.00	500	(7/02)	1.67
Leading Brands (NASDAQ:LBIX)	2.70	400	(8/02)	2.65
Ocean Bio-Chem (NASDAQ:OBCI)	1.60	625	(8/02)	1.59

Original Cost 1/1/92 .... $14,000.00
Proceeds ALL Sales $42.464.51
Portfolio Value 9/20/02 .... $13,888.80
TOTAL VALUE $56,353.31
* Number of shares purchased with $1000.

(The Moneypaper, 930 Mamaroneck Ave., Mamaroneck, NY 10543, 800/388-9993, monthly.)

The One-Month-At-A-Time Deal

This is for the person who doesn't have enough money to buy 12 or 18 of our stocks at one time. Consequently, they buy one stock each month, usually our Company of the Month.

Our Beginner's Portfolio is built on that principal.

Although it is a logical way to dip your toe into the stock market waters, it does require a strong psyche. If, after a few months, the portfolio is worth less than it cost, a feeling of discouragement takes over.

The I-Know-Best Approach

Most of our subscribers probably use this technique. They survey what we have to offer and perhaps do some more research. Then, convinced that their chosen stock will be a winner, they take a big position. Maybe 1,000 or 5,000 shares.

We should be happy about this approach. The investor is making his or her own decisions. Spends time thinking about the stock. And, makes a fairly substantial investment. If it doesn't work out, he or she only have themselves to blame—not us.

Usually, those using this method only have four or five stocks. They ignore the No. 1 Rule in dealing with minipriced issues—diversify. Four or five is not sufficient.

INDIVIDUALS VS. MUTUAL FUNDS

WE HAVE AN AGENDA: WE DON'T LIKE MOST MUTUAL funds.

We have a conflict of interest: *The Bowser Report* is in competition with mutual funds for investor's funds.

In 1980, 267 U.S. mutual funds bought and sold stocks. Today, there are more mutual funds than issues on the New York Stock Exchange.

To give you an idea of how much capital is tied up in stock funds, consider this: The Investment Company Institute announced that in September 2001 holders withdrew $28 billion from the funds. But, *this was only 8% of their total mutual fund holdings.*

The growth of this huge industry centers on two principles: Ignorance of individual investors. The clamor for convenience, even in investing.

Ignorance

The success of the mutual fund industry depends upon its leaders convincing potential buyers they are too ignorant to participate in the stock market by themselves. They don't do this by calling their potential customers dummies. They aren't that crude.

Instead, emphasis is placed on the great skill and professionalism of fund managers. By extension, it would be impossible for you, a lowly slob in the investing business, to equal their great expertise.

In reality, they are professionals only in that they are paid for what they do. Just as a dog catcher can be called a professional because he's compensated for his efforts.

There are no colleges that give degrees in stock picking. This is not a discipline similar to chemistry, biology, medicine, law, etc.

The guiding principle behind stock picking is utterly simple. Review a company's past performance. If it's good, then ask yourself, "Is there an increasing demand for their products and services?" If there is, buy it.

There is no guarantee that the future of any company will be a replay of its past. Management may make a goofy decision. Or, the market for its products or services may go into the dumpster. But, you don't know that ahead of time. Neither does a mutual fund manager.

To buttress its position of invincibility, the securities industry as a whole is guilty of coming up with a language of its own that baffles even brain surgeons. It sounds so impressive.

The basic guidelines for stock market investing are learnable. In a comparatively short period.

Burton Malkiel, an academician, apparently has enough time on his hands that he can study the performance of fund managers. He found that 70% of them underperform the market.

However, you might be someone who says, "Why are you bashing funds? I made money with them." You must be in the 30% mentioned by Prof. Malkiel.

Part of the subtle process of dummying-down investors is to dangle before them a fund's record. Obviously, they only publicize it when their accomplishments are good. But, invariably the big gains were accumulated during bull markets.

The implication is that individuals couldn't have accomplished on their own what was brought forth by the geniuses who manage the funds. . . . In reality, no one knows how well ordinary investors do in the market. No one has ever interviewed all of them—and they number in the millions—to find out if they're successful.

Those fund managers who do well are so few that the top ones are lionized. Peter Lynch comes to mind. . . . Ironically, Mr. Lynch—whom we admire—seems to actually encourage individuals to invest on their own. He certainly gives some excellent advice for doing so. He almost appears to urge the Average Joe to jump in and buy stock on his/her own.

Convenience

The other thing that the mutual fund industry has going for it is the ease of participation. Just send them a check and you're in the game.

Americans love convenience in its many forms. You don't, for example, have to peel, cook and mash potatoes. You can buy a frozen package and in five minutes you have piping hot mashed potatoes, already seasoned.

This convenience comes at a price. First of all, funds have to pay commissions on each transaction, just as do individuals. At one time, because they were buying in such large quantities, they got a big break. But, with the coming of Internet cheap-as-dirt rates, that advantage has almost disappeared.

On top of this, there are management fees. These are the ones used to buy the fund manager's yachts. And, a spokesperson for Vanguard Group, the country's second biggest fund operation, says that when all of the charges are added together, "three percentage points get shaved off the performance of the average fund."

But, probably what irks fund holders the most is the capital gains taxes they have to pay. Every-time a fund sells a stock at a profit, the tax on the gain has to be paid by the holders, even if they didn't own the fund at the time of the transaction.

If a fund has a big turnover rate, the taxes can be considerable. Holders of individual stocks only pay when they personally have benefitted from a capital gain.

Besides the cost disadvantages, fund managers labor under regulatory and marketing restraints that limit flexibility. Individuals don't have such restrictions.

More important than convenience is the pure pleasure that comes from buying and selling individual stocks. It is a creative experience, akin to the excitement that comes from actually painting a picture, rather than just buying one. It is a skill that can be easily acquired and will profitably benefit you the rest of your life.

Finally, we hear people say they don't have time to buy stocks themselves. But, considering the little effort involved, when we hear that complaint, we know we're talking to someone who doesn't manage his time well.

Conclusion

Human nature being what it is, the huge army of mutual fund investors will continue marching forward.

The mutual fund industry has had its ups-and-downs. In the 1960s it did well. But, in the 1970s it suffered badly, only regaining momentum with the bull market of the 1980s and 1990s.

Too, we should be specific. We are talking about open-end mutual funds that buy back shares from investors who wish to sell. We are not writing about closed-end funds that have a limited number of shares. Closed-end funds trade as though they were individual stocks.

We also concede there are mutual funds that operate in areas in which the Average Joe doesn't have sufficient information to buy the security itself, such as on the international scene.

Also, ordinary investors do not have the necessary details to buy and sell certain bonds. Municipal bonds are a tricky area, and a fund manager who is studying them all day has an advantage. (The Editor owns municipal bond funds.)

But, as for open-end mutual funds, our concluding pitch comes from James Cramer. He's the irascible money manager who is all over TV and the Internet.

"I know some of you out there may be wondering why a professional money manager like myself would write a story telling people they can do just fine without help from folks like me.

"My answer: We all can go to Home Depot, get the materials, have the tools and fix pretty much whatever we want these days. Yet carpenters, builders and electricians have work to do.

"Some people don't like to do things themselves. For them, I do the trick. But, for the do-it-yourselfers, the Home Depot is cheaper, more satisfying and, for the craftsmen among you, better."

Note: The editor knows something about mutual fund managers. In the early 1980s he managed the Bowser Growth Fund in addition to publishing The Bowser Report. *The fund was absorbed by an English group. It no longer exists.*

WHOM WOULD YOU BET WITH?

INVESTOR A HAS A VERITABLE trading desk at her fingertips. She knows her risk profile. She buys only stocks she loves (a handful is plenty) and knows she can hold them for as long as she wishes (giving her control over her tax fate). She does not have to fret about how she's doing month-to-month and does not have to buy the stocks everyone else is buying,  just to prove she can pick winners. If she can't find a stock she likes, she doesn't buy anything at all. *She is today's individual investor.*

INVESTOR B IS INUNDATED WITH feedback and information. He has to take risks, sometimes outrageous ones, just to keep pace with his peers. He must keep much of his cash in the market, whether he wants to or not, and he must contort himself, Houdini-like, at the end of every quarter, to show he has heard of the latest investing fads, even when he knows little or nothing about them. He pays capital gains taxes every November, whether it makes strategic sense or not. He is a mutual fund manager.

– James Cramer in *Worth Magazine*, May 1997

START YOUR OWN MUTUAL FUND

OH, THOSE WONDERFUL MUTUAL FUND MANAGERS—SO intelligent, so market savvy.

Or, are they? They have gains in bull markets and losses in bear markets. . . . Why pay big bucks for that kind of service?

According to the Feb. 25, 2002 *Barron's*: "From 1984 through 2000, when the S&P 500 Stock Index racked up an average annual return of 16.3%, the average equity mutual fund investor wound up with a yearly return of 5.32%."

Recently we were in a bear market comparable to that of 1973-74, which was the time to reassess your position in the market. But, those bad days have ended. The market has resumed its growth. It always does!

So, start your own mutual fund. Let us pick the stocks. You follow the Bowser Game Plan. The management fee is $54 year—the cost of a subscription to *The Bowser Report*. And, a little of your time.

A frequently cited reason for buying mutual funds is that they provide diversity. They buy a whole bunch of stocks. . . . You can easily do that on your own. It doesn't cost much to buy 12 to 18 of our little ones.

Andrew Tobias is a noted financial author. In March 1997, he listed 10 reasons for not buying an equity mutual fund. His third reason: "*You'll miss out on tiny stocks too small for funds.* Few mutual funds can invest in small companies. For one thing, it's just not worth their time. For another, buying— and eventually selling—$1 million worth of some small, illiquid company is bound to drive the price up (and then down), making it very expensive to get in and out.

"But, some of the best opportunities lie in these microcaps. The little guy, with his or her 100-share or 500-share stake, can slip in and out like a pickpocket."

And, there are many other reasons to shy away from stock mutual funds. Primarily, there is the matter of fees, which never stop, even if your fund is performing badly.

Transaction costs: The average stock fund has a portfolio turnover of 72% a year. (These trading costs eat into profits.) A fund manager pays a commission to a brokerage firm on each buy and sale just like you do. You'll have fewer transactions.

What fund companies charge for management fees may not seem like much, but they add up. On average they take $1.54 in fees for every $100 invested in equity funds, up 14% since 1993, according to mutual fund tracker Lipper, Inc.

Some mutual fund investors face steep tax bills —for capital gains on stocks bought months or years before they became shareholders. But, as operator of your own mutual fund, you'll only pay income taxes on the transactions you actually make.

And, if you want to get out of a fund, there can be a fee. *The Wall Street Journal* (7/5/02) noted that D. Royce Boyer, a retired music professor, sold mutual fund shares that declined to about $60,000 in value. "It cost me about $1,600 to get out," the 67-year-old investor said.

James K. Glassman, the famous financial author, doesn't like stock mutual funds. He wrote: "My own theory for their dismal performance is that fund managers, operating under perverse incentives, can not operate the way intelligent individual investors can.

"Managers are hyperactive because they have to show strong short-term returns—otherwise they cannot attract or hold antsy investors. They can't buy a great underpriced company and wait five years for it to bloom. If they did, they'd lose their jobs.

"If the market crashes, most mutual fund managers will have to sell stocks to raise cash to meet the redemption demands of their shareholders. But, at the same time, individual investors are buying stocks at bargain prices. Mutual funds don't have that luxury."

As we've indicated, mutual funds have more fees than a dog has fleas. For example, there are switching fees, which some fund families assess when you sell shares of one fund and use the proceeds to buy another one in the same family. . . . Switching fees are there to discourage market timers.

Then there are 12b-1 fees which are deducted from a fund to finance marketing and shareholder services.

The people who run these funds do well personally with your money. The average compensation for the CEO of a fund company was $1 million. Reportedly, top fund managers at Fidelity earned more than half a million. (These are 1996 figures. You can well imagine what they are making now.)

The best reason we know of for you to operate your own mutual fund—with our help—is this:

> NO ONE CARES ABOUT YOUR MONEY QUITE AS MUCH AS YOU DO.

Give us a try. Maybe start on a small scale. If it doesn't work out, you can take two actions:

(1) Cuss us out.

(2) Stop subscribing to *The Bowser Report*.

BOWSER MICROCAP STOCK INDEX

JOHN PICCHIETTI IS A YOUNG STOCK TRADER WHO operates in the Chicago area. For some time, John insisted that we capitalize on our unique database of microcap stocks. And, that we should develop an index that reflects the fluctuation in the value of these small companies.

The database he refers to is *The Bowser Directory of Small Stocks*. It's more than a collection of 600 to 700 small stocks. There are 14 fields of information on each stock.

But, what is unique is that each one is given a Bowser Rating. That means that those suitable for buying are identified. Thus, we have a mini-analysis of each issue.

An index of minipriced stocks is worthwhile for these reasons:

(1) An index of truly small companies does not exist. The Russell 2000, which is billed as a small-stock index, has stocks with market capitalizations of $1 billion or more.

(2) It provides a snapshot of how this section of the market is doing.

(3) It offers a degree of legitimacy to so-called penny stocks. And, legitimacy and acceptance are things they badly need.

(4) A stock exchange could adopt the index and make it possible for investors to buy this basket of

microcaps just as though they were buying one share of stock.

So that the index is built on sound principles, we sought the help of George K. Zestos, Associate Professor of Economics at Christopher Newport University, which is located near our office. As an economist, Dr. Zestos is familiar with the mechanics of the stock market. In fact, he's taught a workshop for Virginia teachers on the "Stock Market Game."

Some ground rules were established, such as:

(1) The value of the index will be computed each month.

(2) Issues to be included will have a Bowser Rating (BR) of 8 or higher and a price of $3 or less.

(3) The index will be composed of 50 stocks.

(4) The first month's computation will be the baseline. Each succeeding computation will be compared to the baseline.

(5) The status of the index will be reported each month in *The Bowser Report*, but a full breakdown—company by company—will appear in each edition of *The Bowser Directory of Small Stocks*.

(6) If a stock ceases to trade because the company has been bought out—or for any other reason—it will be replaced with another issue that has a BR of 8 or higher.

Dr. Zestos suggested a weighted index, which reflects the total worth of each stock. And, to accomplish this, on a specified date, the market capitalization of each company is determined by multiplying the stock price by the number of shares outstanding.

The market capitalization for each of the 50 stocks is added to get a grand total. Then, each stock's market capitalization is divided by the grand total. This gives the weight for each stock.

Finally, to construct the Bowser Microcap Stock Index, we multiply the weight by the respective prices of all 50 stocks and then add up the 50 results. . . . To clarify even further, this is the step-by-step process:

(1) The stock price of each issue is multiplied by the number of shares outstanding. This gives the market capitalization. This, in other words, is what the market thinks the company is worth.

(2) The market capitalization of all 50 stocks is added.

(3) The market capitalization of each stock is divided by the grand total. For example, Abatix Corp.'s stock price was $2.05 on 8/9/01—multiplied by 1,700,000 shares outstanding—gives a figure of $3,485,000, its market capitalization on that date.

(4) The market capitalization for Abatix of $3,485,000 is divided by the grand total capitalization of $978,113,000. This gives a figure of .0036. This is the baseline number.

(5) Abatix's number of .0036 is multiplied by the current stock price ($2.05), giving a new number of .0074. Each month, the new stock price will be multiplied by .0036, the baseline number.

(6) The Abatix number of .0074 will be added to the similar number for the other 49 stocks. The sum of the 50 is multiplied by 100 (a multiplier) to give the index number.

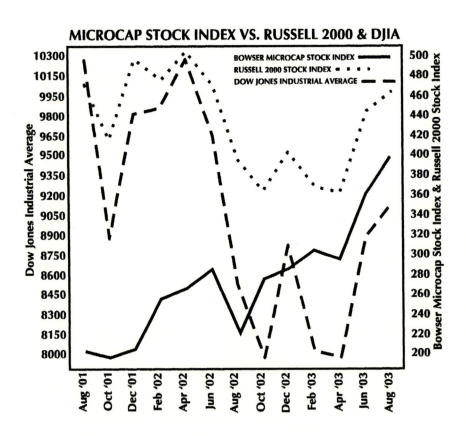

44 – Guaranteed Profits With Small Stocks

Bowser Microcap Stock Index
(Prices used as of 9/02/03)

APPAREL/FRAGRANCES
Alpha Pro Tech .0420
Parlux Fragrance .1038

ENVIRONMENTAL
Abatix .0153
Entrx Corp.(A) .0159
Perma-Fix(B) .1510
Synagro Tech .1094

FINANCIAL
Capital Title .1929

FOOD
Stake Tech .2986
Pyramid Brew(C) .0682
Tofutti Brands .0389
Vita Food Products .0750

MANUFACTURING
Chad Therapeutics(D) .0493
Cohesant Tech .0233
Emerson Radio .2029
Everlast Worldwide .0184
Hi-Shear Tech(E) .0581
Pure World .0141

MARKETING/WHOLESALE
Leather Factory .1215
Reconditioned Systems .0070
Reliv Int'l .0546

MEDICAL
Amer Medical Alert .0583
Compex Tech(F) .2155
Dialysis Corp .0230
Dynatronics .0098
Escalon Medical .0316
Immucell .0196
Int'l Remote Imaging .0818
Oralabs Holding .0118
Penn Treaty Amer(G) .0989
Trinity Biotech .2690

NATURAL RESOURCES
Contango Oil & Gas(H) .1401
Delta Petroleum(I) .1136
Dynamic Oil & Gas .1211
Equity Oil Company .1080
ENGlobal Corp(J) .1407

Exploration Co. .2901
Harvest Nat'l Resources (K) .3390

PRISON MANAGEMENT
Avalon Correctional .0152

RETAIL/GIFTS/HOTELS
Action Products .0064
Backyard Burger .0492
Creative Host Services .0173
Zaneti Inc.(L) .0137
Rag Shops .0493

TECHNOLOGY
Canterbury Consulting(M) .0028
Digital Recorders(N) .0159
Elecsys .0100
Franklin Elec Pub(O) .0660
Lan Vision Systems(P) .0458
Wireless Telecom .1107
SI Technologies(Q) .0127

GRAND TOTAL 4.1475 X 100 = 414.75

(A) – Was Metalclad. (B) – Replaced Rent-A-Wreck of America, which was delisted. (C) – Replaced Collector's Universe, which The Bowser Report recommended be sold. (D) – Replaced Allied Devices (delisted). (E) – Replaced Alternate Marketing Networks (delisted). (F) – Was Rehabilicare Inc. (G) – Replaced Biospecifics Tech (delisted) (H) – Replaced Intelligent Controls, which was acquired by Franklin Electric Dec '01. (I) Replaced e.Mergent, which was acquired by Clear One Communications Jun '02. (J) Replaced Sel Leb Marketing, which was delisted. (K) – Was Benten Oil & Gas. (L) – Was BAB Holdings, then Planet Zanett, now Zanett, Inc. (M) – 1-for-7 reverse split 1/24/03. (N) – Replaced Technisource, Inc., which was acquired by IntelliMark Dec '01. (O) Replaced Magellan Petroleum, which was delisted. (P) Replaced DG Jewelry, which was delisted. (Q) – Replaced Janus Hotels/Resorts, which The Bowser Report recommended be sold.

LIES! LIES! LIES!

WALL STREET IS UNDER SIEGE BECAUSE THEIR ANALYSTS fabricated research reports during the dot.com/hi-tech bubble. Put simply, they lied.

And, all of this lying took place with the approval of the huge brokerage firms. The big bosses established the groundwork for these fabrications.

That they lied is not surprising to us. Major and regional brokerage firms have been lying for years about penny stocks. They brazenly encourage their employees in offices throughout the nation to say that all penny stocks are worthless. Even those of companies with rising earnings and sales.

Lying should not be an integral part of a company's way of doing business. As in personal life, it causes trouble.

Thousands of individual investors blindly relied on these brokerage firms for advice. It cost them, collectively, billions of dollars. Now, these brokerage firms are having to pay millions upon millions in response to regulatory actions/lawsuits.

Just as innocent Enron employees are suffering for the digressions of their bosses, so are hordes of hard-working, honest brokers. In our three decades in this business, we've come to know many of them. But, unfortunately, there are rotten apples. Just as there are bad doctors, lawyers and—investment newsletter editors.

That big investment houses are prejudiced against tiny minipriced stocks is well known. Here we explore this phenomenon some more.

Ironically, the promotion by the big houses of high-priced stocks, regardless of whether they warrant promotion, is having a backlash. Many investors are turning to microcaps that are producing profits.

There is only one reason why so many in the securities industry demonize microcaps. They cannot make money selling them. But, they put up a big smokescreen of phony reasons as to why they don't want you to buy them. We expose those reasons below.

Litigation

For years we've been faithfully reading *The Wall Street Journal* and *Investor's Business Daily*. Plus *Barron's*, *Forbes*, *Business Week*, *Money* and *Kiplinger's*. But, we haven't seen a report on a disgruntled buyer of a $2 stock suing his broker. The threat of lawsuits is just another fabrication by big brokerage firms for not selling minipriced stocks.

Manipulation

With its vast network of brokers, Merrill Lynch is handicapped. If it had all of its account executives recommending a company with only three million shares and a $2 share price—well, the stock price would be artificially rocketed up.

However, for a stock to be truly manipulated, someone has to do the manipulation. It's hardly ever these tiny companies themselves. Even though they might want to manipulate their shares upward—they don't legally have the means or the knowledge.

The manipulation that has been done in recent years has been the work of rogue brokerages. These are firms that could be thwarted by the ethical operators in the industry. New brokerage firms should be placed on at least a two- or three-year probation during their initial existence to make sure they are operating ethically.

All Penny Stocks Are Worthless

We've disproved this lie. For years. All you have to do is review our Historical Review to see what happened to every issue we recommended. Many were big winners. (To receive a FREE copy of the latest Historical Review, send a self-addressed, stamped [60¢] number 10 envelope to *The Bowser Report*, P.O. Box 6278, Newport News, VA 23606 and a copy will be zipped right out to you.)

The Compliance Officer

In each brokerage branch office there is an individual whose purpose in life is to enforce the firm's ethical standards. Such as making sure a broker doesn't sell a 20-year bond to a 94-year-old widow who just inherited $100,000. But, it looks to us that the compliance officer's life is dedicated to making sure a broker doesn't recommend a $2 stock. . . . The compliance officer can be easily recognized. He or she wears a halo.

Why did you buy that $2 stock?

The Templeton Caper

In the 1/21/02 *Forbes*, columnist John W. Rogers, Jr. reminded us of John Templeton. In 1939, World War II had just broken out in Europe. Uncertainty plagued the U.S. stock market.

The then-young Tennessean bought $100 worth of every stock on the New York and American stock exchanges selling for $1.00 or less. He even borrowed $10,000 to help buy the shares of 104 companies, 34 of them bankrupt.

If the same scenario were repeated today, the compliance officer would have yelled at the broker who made the sales, "You idiot. That nut will lose all of his money. And, you know damn well that such a sale is against our policy."

As the youthful Templeton anticipated, America's economy rebounded strongly. The famed investor held on for an average of four years and quadrupled his purchase price.

Randall W. Forsyth in *Barron's*

"You may not catch Microsoft in its early stages as a penny stock. But, you might find some gems undiscovered by Wall Street. And, given the Street's sorry performance following erstwhile blue chips, it is hard to argue that penny stocks are much riskier." (*April 22, 2002, page T5*)

Small Investors Are Incompetent?

"Most folks can invest successfully on their own. However, Wall Street desperately tries to persuade small investors they are utterly incompetent in all things financial. Thereby driving them into the costly embrace of investment advisors.

"But, here's the amazing part: Many investment advisers seem to believe this propaganda. Why? Maybe it's a reflection of their clientele. Who ends up using brokers and financial planners? Often it is folks who messed up royally on their own and desperately need help.

"But, just because some investors mess up does not mean they are all incompetent. Advisors, nevertheless, rarely meet more-competent investors, because these folks don't seek help." (*Jonathan Clements*, The Wall Street Journal, *April 24, 2002*)

Maniacal Hatred of Penny Stocks

This hatred by major and big regional firms was best demonstrated to us when we wanted to interview a broker with one of these firms.

He is a long-time subscriber to *The Bowser Report* and a truly outstanding individual. We know him well enough that we can confirm that the welfare of his clients is a guiding principle. And, he has enough common sense to know that some minipriced stocks can be profitable.

We wanted to interview him for a front-page article. But, his company required that public appearances of any kind be cleared by headquarters.

Our interview was turned down. And, the big bosses said if he did contribute to a publication that endorses penny stocks he would be fired. Even though he is one of the firm's biggest producers.

Small Stocks Are Beautiful

"Only a few years ago, 'Big is beautiful,' was the mantra of Wall Street. Stocks of large companies, with their global reach, financial power and experienced management teams, were bound to outshine shares of small companies.

"But, as is often the case when seemingly everyone is in agreement, the conventional wisdom is wrong. For the past two years, small-company stocks have been the ones to own. There's no reason to expect the trend to reverse." (Kiplinger's, April 2002)

Wall Street to Small Investors: Scram!

"Wall Street has got a lot less friendly toward small investors, especially those who are do-it-yourselfers. Down the road, I think they'll regret it. A lot of these small investors would have grown to profitable customers." (Scott Cooley, editor of Morningstar Mutual Funds, a Chicago newsletter, December 2001)

Where Can the Small Investor Go?

As has been noted, for all intents and purposes, the big brokerage houses have abandoned the small investor. . . . Fortunately, the stock market is served by others than the giant Wall Street outfits. There are hundreds of small brokerages that welcome the $2 investor. And, the online brokers never ask questions regarding the stocks you're buying. They just want the transaction.

Never Say Sell

In the research departments of the giant Wall Street firms you have grown men and women intently studying corporations. But, when they see a company collapsing before their eyes, they can't warn the firm's clients with a sell recommendation.

This is the ultimate in lying. (One UBS Paine-Webber stock advisor who recommended selling Enron in Aug '01 was immediately fired.) . . . What can you expect from analysts who are only working for minimum wages? (In their cases, the minimum starts at $100,000 annually and goes up to $20 million.)

WHY THEY DON'T LIKE PENNY STOCKS

UP UNTIL THE EARLY 1980S, SHARES SELLING FOR LESS than $1 apiece were just another category of stocks. They were speculative. But, there wasn't the mass derision about them that now exists in stock market circles.

In the 1970s and early 1980s penny stock brokerages proliferated. Mostly in Denver. Many of them were unscrupulous, to say the least. Probably the most notorious was Meyer Blinder of Blinder Robinson & Co. . . . sometimes referred to as "Blind 'em & Rob 'em."

The U.S. Securities & Exchange Commission stepped in, together with state regulators. Now there are hardly any IPOs with shares priced less than $1. (We know of only one recently.)

A lot of bad press didn't help to brand penny stocks with a good image. And, dot.coms and telecoms have sunk into the penny price range, which hasn't helped this category, either.

Although there can be extraneous factors, such as a change in industry practices, the primary reason stocks these days are quoted for less than $1 is due to poor management. Invariably these are companies that are losing money.

Now the SEC considers any stock under $5 a penny stock. So, there are lots of 'em. But, among them are many jewels.

JOE VIDEMSEK

When we called Joe Videmsek in Twinsburg, Ohio, to tell him he had been selected as *The Bowser Report* Investor of the Year, he responded, "I'm overwhelmed. But, why me? Usually you pick college graduates. I'm just an ordinary 'Joe'."

Well, this gentleman is far from ordinary. He's managed his own finances so astutely that some so-called "experts" could learn from him. Perhaps it's due to his affinity for numbers.

Born in Cleveland, Ohio, in 1937, Joe graduated from St. Joseph High School in that city. That was followed by 10 years in cost accounting at Black & Decker. And then 23 years in the purchasing department at Automated Packaging.

In Oct '63 he married Theresa Enders. There is a running joke in the family that he married an older woman. (Theresa is eight days older than Joe.)

Theresa held various positions during her working career. But, what is most unusual is that both quit their jobs when they were 59½. Thus, they entered retirement without the benefit of pensions.

Their six years of retirement have been buttressed by dividends from blue chip stocks that Joe bought during his working career, Social Security (when he reached 62) and his skill as a sweepstakes player (see page 45). But, their primary source has been the profits garnered from investing in Bowser stocks.

We visited with Joe and Theresa in August 2002 at their home south of Cleveland. Below is our interview. . . . WE SALUTE OUR 2002 INVESTOR OF THE YEAR!

BOWSER: *HOW LONG HAVE YOU BEEN BUYING STOCKS?*

Videmsek: Since I turned 21.

How did that happen?

Joe Videmsek

An aunt encouraged me to buy stocks that paid a cash dividend.

But, now you don't acquire dividend-paying stocks? Right?

Today we use the capital gains we get with your stocks to supplement our income in retirement.

You and Theresa have an active retirement.

The profits from your stocks finance some of our trips. We make about 30 a year. Plus, they help to pay other expenses, including medical insurance.

Why do you like low-priced stocks?

Leverage. You can buy 100 shares of a $30 stock for $3,000. With that same $3,000 you can buy 1,000 shares of a $3 stock.

It seems that Wall Street is convinced the higher the price of a stock, the safer it is.

The potential for a big loss on an $80 or $90 stock is tremendous. And, now we're seeing a lot of examples of that. Some of those are currently selling for $15 or $10 or less.

You can also lose with microcaps.

Of course. If you buy at $3 and it goes to $2, you get out. On $1,000, you lose $333—not many thousands of dollars.

How about losing with a portfolio of minipricers?

To use round numbers, if you have 10, three may go down and three may go up. But, you still have four that can make money later on. You can't beat that.

You didn't become interested in minipriced stocks until you subscribed to The Bowser Report?

Previously I had an interest but never did anything about it.

How many stocks do you own?

Forty-six. Sixteen are Bowser issues. The rest are the dividend-paying ones that I accumulated over the years.

What do you do with the dividends now?

Once a year we take some of the cash that had accumulated in our dividend account and put it in our current budget.

Up until you retired, you let the cash generated in the dividend-paying stocks accumulate. In other words, that was compounding. It was your own dividend reinvesting program.

By the way, I should also point out that with the proceeds from the sale of Bowser stocks we buy more Bowser issues.

At first, weren't you skeptical of low-priced stocks? After all, you had been living in an investment world populated by major corporations.

Not really. However, at first I only bought 100 shares at a time. Then, five or six months later, I realized what was going on, so I started buying 200, 500 and more.

How many do you now buy?

One thousand shares of each Company of the Month. Once in a while I will buy more. I bought 1,000 of Monterey Pasta at $1.25 and then a second thousand at $3.00.

What features do you like best about The Bowser Report?

I like the feedback I get. Admittedly, there isn't a lot of information published in our local newspapers and the financial press on these stocks. But, I know if there is a big development about one of my stocks, *The Bowser Report* will have it. . . .

With the performance of your Bowser stocks, have you ever brought it down to a yearly percentage?

Not really. I know I'm making money. I know it is higher than 10%.

What do you think of our Microcap Stock Index?

It's good for new people coming into your program who want the assurance that your stocks have a yearly percentage gain.

Do you follow the Bowser Game Plan?

If I put some of your stocks in my IRA, I do follow the Plan. But, in my regular account, if a stock goes down 20% from its most recent high, I sell all of it.

Go over that again.

In my regular account, if I buy at $3 and it goes up to $7 and then retreats 20%, I sell all of it. In the IRA, if

I buy at $3 and it rises to $6, I'll sell half. The remainder I will sell if it drops 25% from its most recent high.

Have you sold a stock and after you sold, it goes back up?

Yes. But, I don't rebuy because I've already made a profit on it.

How do you feel about losses?

You have to have discipline. You have to take losses, because that's part of the game. You can't get 10 out of 10. But, following your procedure, it's no sweat.

Do you get emotionally upset when you have a loss?

Are you kidding? I'm past that. Once I sell a stock, I don't continue to follow it.

What have been your best Bowser stocks?

Comtech Telecommunications was great. Monterey Pasta has also been good to me. Now it's $8.25, but if it drops to $7, I'll sell. Sold Air Methods at $8.25.

What was your worst Bowser stock?

Aztec Tech Partners.

That's a stock we recommended in 1999. It was part of the bubble and when the bubble burst, down it went. How about recent action?

Of the eight stocks I've bought this year, the only one that hasn't worked out was InfoNow. I sold at $1.50.

Obviously, you are patient with these equities.

With a lot of these companies, if you hold them three years, then you are doing OK. Look at Monterey Pasta. That was a Company of the Month in '98.

So, you don't have a high level of expectation.

You can't buy one of your stocks and expect it to double in three months.

Your broker is Charles Schwab and obviously you are satisfied with the firm. What is the commission you pay?

$29.50. To me it's worth it. The service is good and I can get a quote whenever I want one. [Editor's Note: Since our interview, Mr. Videmsek has changed brokers. He now uses Brown & Co. (866/502-7696).]

What do people say when you tell them you're buying penny stocks?

I can't convince 'em to buy your stocks.* I can show them my record and they still won't do it.

Why is that?

I think the media has brainwashed people about penny stocks. And, they've done a good job. People are scared of them. I think they are one of the better investments.

---

* In the book, *Meet The Millionaire Next Door*, is a formula to compute your net worth. Using that formula, Joe has determined that Theresa's and his net worth is $35,000 more than when they retired.

FORMER INVESTORS OF THE YEAR
1996 –Chuck Bostrom
　　　Lewiston, MT
1997 –Rose Marie Bienick
　　　Elmwood Park, NJ
　　　(Deceased)
1998 –Roger J. Bakken
　　　Saint Paul, MN
1999 –Linda Mullin
　　　Philadelphia, PA
2000 –Bose Agnew
　　　Washington, CD
2001 –David Rhodes
　　　Chesapeake, VA
　　　(Deceased)

Joe – the Sweepstakes Expert

IN 1963, OUR INVESTOR OF THE YEAR HAD JUST JOINED the ranks of the married when he submitted his first sweepstakes entry. And, won. A waffle iron. (They still use it.)

Three months later he entered an RCA contest. And, won. A stereo. (They still have it.)

"Wow! I must be on to something!" Scroll forward to 2002. By now he's participated in at least 4,000 sweepstakes. About 100 a year.

Joe and Theresa's life has been enriched with all sorts of free trips and merchandise. The latest big prize is a brand new Ford Taurus.

Another memorable win was an all-expense-paid round trip to Paris on the Concorde. And, included in the package was a stay at an exclusive hotel. One that had served as headquarters of the German high command during the World War II German occupation of France.

Joe Videmsek with a sweepstakes prize

While there is a great deal of luck involved, Mr. Videmsek shared with us two simple principles that are essential in winning sweepstakes.

(1) Read the rules very closely. Follow them precisely. . . . Many entries are losers from the very beginning because they use the wrong address.

(2) Joe showed us the envelopes for two entries he was ready to mail. One was covered with 37 one-cent stamps. The other had one 37-cent stamp, but red lines were drawn at an angle across the front of the envelope. . . . Anything to legally attract attention.

NOTE: Mr. Videmsek does not enter essay-type sweepstakes. You know—"I like Smith's Shoe Polish because . . ." Instead, he participates in the type in which you just submit a coupon.

YOU NEED AN EXIT STRATEGY

THE BUY-AND-HOLD THEORY MAY HAVE WORKED WITH CocaCola at one time. But, it hasn't recently.

And, it never has worked that way with minipriced stocks.

You have to sell when you have a reasonable profit. And, you have to sell when there is no possibility of a gain. You need an exit strategy.

Actually, this applies to all stocks regardless of their prices. In fact, if those poor souls who bought the dot.coms and telecoms during the bubble had followed our Selling Plan, they would all have money in their coffers today.

In one sense, this is a hindsight observation. However, since 1982 we have been advocating that you sell when a stock doubles from your purchase price. Sell the remainder when your shares drop 25% from their most recent high. We also tell you to sell when the performance of an issue deteriorates.

Not surprisingly, a deterrent to using a prescribed exit strategy is the fear the holder will miss out on a bigger gain if the stock price continues to go up.

And, that is a possibility. But, statistically, the chance of these minipriced ones going to $50 is very slight. . . . We have the figures.

Since 1977, we have recommended 477 issues, of which 3.6% have soared 500% or more. The bulk of the rest of our picks showed smaller gains. But, when these are added up, you have a nice pot of money.

> Mark Twain was one of this country's greatest humorists. He was also an entrepreneur. A frustrated one. He invested in several "hare-brained" schemes. But, the one that almost put him in the poorhouse was a type-setting machine that never proved to be practical. . . . However, if Mr. Twain were alive today, his speculative urge could be satisfied merely by following the Bowser Game Plan, which would make him money.

BUCKAROO MEMO: WALL STREET'S MANTRA – "BUY HIGH"

YOU HEAR IT CONSTANTLY ON CNBC. MONEY managers harp on it. Writers in big financial publications are obsessed with it. . . . It's their mantra: *Buy high quality stocks.*

Invariably, they mean high-priced equities.

We were reminded of this by something that Michael Burke wrote in his guest column in *The Moneypaper.* . . . Incidentally, Michael is one of the wise men in the investment advisory business. In his day job, he's editor of *Investor's Intelligence* (914/632-0422), which is a technically oriented newsletter.

Here's what Michael observed:

"In its Aug. 14, 2000 issue, *Fortune* magazine featured an article entitled, '10 Stocks to Last the Decade.' *Fortune* reported that after relying on its own due diligence to choose these wonderful stocks, it also enlisted the advice of some of the best stock-picking managers in the country.

"The magazine noted that if you are a long-term investor, these stocks should stand your retirement account in good stead. The 10 stocks, together with their prices on the day after the article was published, were:

Nokia $40.125
Enron $82.125
Broadcom $245.875
Univision $47.438
Genentech $82.65

Nortel $80.312
Oracle $40.625
Viacom $70.00
Charles Schwab $37.75
Morgan Stanley $101.50

"An investment of $1,000 into each of these back then would have left you with very little. Your $1,000 in Enron is now worthless, and the amount in Nortel is now worth $97.11. The other stocks also dropped, with huge losses in Oracle, Broadcom and Schwab."

"We'll hit the shareholders with more stock options."

70 – Guaranteed Profits With Small Stocks

BOWSER RATINGS

WE DISCUSS IN DETAIL THE BOWSER RATING SYSTEM IN our book, *Making Dollars With Pennies*. This is just a quick overview. . . . We rate 12 factors, one of which is double-weighted. This means the highest score any stock can receive is 13. In the many years we've lived with the Ratings, only two or three stocks have warranted a 13. . . . If a stock gets an 8 or higher, we consider it a buy. That is a subjective verdict, however, as are many aspects of these ratings. Too, you will note that the factors are balance sheet-oriented. Finally, it should be noted that this effort is not aimed at trying to determine which stocks will appreciate the most. It is an effort to separate the financially strong issues from the weak ones. The 12 factors:

No. 1: Book Value. If you take the shareholder's equity (minus the value of any preferred stock) and divide it by the number of shares outstanding, you get book value. For an "X," it should be more than the current stock price.

No. 2: Principal Business. From time to time certain categories of business are "hot." In the 1960s conglomerates were popular. At other times it has been energy, high tech, etc. Many times, even though a company's performance is poor, because they're in this "hot" business, their stock will do well. On the other hand, if a firm is doing well in most other aspects and it is not in an industry that is popular, we will give it an "X" for business.

No. 3: Sales. Although we deal with small companies, being too small is a negative factor. To get an "X" they must have annual revenues of $5 million or more.

No: 4: Highest Price Per Share in Last Two Years. If a stock has been double its current price in the last two years, it gets an "X." In other words, we want to know if the stock can move.

No. 5: Average Daily Volume. If a stock is not frequently traded, then obviously there is not much demand for it. We insist that—to get an "X" in this category—it have a daily average trading volume of at least 600 shares.

No. 6: Dividend. If there has been a recent cash dividend, the stock earns an "X." Just the ability to pay such a dividend indicates that the firm's finances are in good shape.

No. 7: Current Ratio. This is the relationship between current assets and current liabilities. The minimum that we accept is 1.8 to 1, meaning that for every $1.80 of current assets there is $1.00 of current liabilities. The greater the ratio, the greater the working capital.

No. 8: Long-Term Debt. We say (again, strictly subjectively) that if the long-term debt is more than 10% of annual sales, it is excessive and does not warrant an "X."

No. 9: No. of Shares Outstanding. Stock price is the product of supply and demand. If there are too many shares (supply) and not enough demand (buyers), the stock won't do well. If a company has sales up to $5 million annually, there should be no more than 1 million shares outstanding. For up to $10 million, no more than 1.5 million, etc.

No. 10: Earnings Last Five Years. With small stocks we are concerned with growth. We are interested in profits. We hope for an upward trend over a five-year period, but even a shorter upward trend of the past two years gets an "X."

No. 11: Current-Earnings. As we said, profits are important. That's why corporations are created. If the current earnings are better than those of a year ago, this is the factor that is double-weighted—two "Xs."

No. 12: Current Sales. We are looking for growth in both sales and earnings. So, an increase in current sales compared to the previous year is good for an "X."

OUR $5,000 GUARANTEE

Offer

In three years, after following our Game Plan Rules explicitly, if you do not make money, R. Max Bowser will personally pay you $5,000 in cash. (We can not say what your portfolio will be, since not everyone will be buying the same stocks at the same time. People will begin the program at different times.)

Timing

This offer does not involve backdating, such as someone saying they invested in our stocks between 1998 and 2001. The three-year period begins with the first Bowser stock purchased after November 18, 2002. Through the years we have been clarifying our Game Plan Rules. It was only recently that we emphasized Proceeds from Sales as being important in determining portfolio value.

Documentation

When making a claim, submit confirmation forms on each purchase and sale. The claim must be presented so that it is easily comprehended.

Tactics

This offer pertains only to our recommendations. . . . Three years are involved because our stocks often require a comparatively long time to develop and prosper.

THOUGHTS ON OUR $5,000 GUARANTEE

OUR $5,000 GUARANTEE IS VERY UNUSUAL. WE DO NOT know of any other investment newsletter that has made a similar offer. We most certainly have not heard of a brokerage firm that is so confident of its advice that such a guarantee is provided.

Disciplined Investing

The Bowser Game Plan Rules offer a disciplined approach to stock market investing. It removes emotion from the entire process.

We had a caller last month who is still holding Clear One Communications, even though at one time it was over $20 a share. . . . "Why didn't you follow our Selling Plan? . . ."

"I think it is such a good company that I did not want to part with it."

Of course, he passed up a lot of profit! And, while it is admittedly one of our better firms, he could have bought back in at a low price. In fact, recently it stopped trading in reaction to allegations by the U.S. Securities & Exchange Commission. . . . Our caller's approach defeats the goal of making money in a disciplined investment program.

Ironically, if an investor sells and the stock turns around and goes up, then he's upset. That one incident is all he needs to convince himself that the Selling Plan is no good.

No human activity is infallible. But, our program is statistically viable. We know that 90% of the time our Selling Plan works.

Your Own Market Analyst

There is a little bit of stock market analyst in all of us. And, if the truth is to be told, any of you reading this could be a full-time analyst. This is not an activity that has Einstein-type complexities.

Yet, we are witness to the suffering of those who decided they were the masters of the stock market. For example, we had a voice on the phone who admitted to being the agonized holder of 10,000 shares of International Remote Imaging Systems. He wasn't a *Bowser Report* subscriber, but he heard we had recommended IRI. He was gasping for every little particle of IRI information he could find. . . . He had put all of his apples in one basket.

Anticipation

Another failing is the expectation that every stock we pick is a winner. . . . No analyst rings a bell every time. . . . A company's future may entail a change in tactics, management eruption or a transformation of its marketplace. . . . This is the area in which we lose a lot of people. They buy two, three or four Companies of the Month. After four months their stocks haven't appreciated. They become discouraged. "This isn't working. I could have done better with a bank savings account."

That's why in our $5,000 guarantee we specify that you stay with us three years. The calendar is on our side. The longer you stick with our mini-priced wonders, the better you will do—if you follow the Game Plan.

Research

The key to successful stock market investing is having available a mass of information on the companies that intrigue you. . . . That is where we have an advantage over Mr. Six Pack, who is picking stocks at home. We probably have the largest database of stocks that are $3 or less—each of which has been analyzed as evidenced by its Bowser Rating.

Another factor in our favor is that we devote full time to managing our database and picking stocks. . . . In other words, let us do the research.

The Cost

Life can be cruel. Nothing is free. You need to spend $54 a year for a *Bowser Report*. But, something much more precious is involved. Your time. . . . Not that following the Game Plan is a guzzler of hours. However, it does call for you to be on your toes. . . . Some of our stocks can shoot up overnight. And, you want to capture one when it doubles. . . . This means you can't check your stocks only once a week—you may miss an important uptick.

"You want to know what the stock market is going to do? Hey, I'm good, but I'm not that good."

REACTION TO THE $5,000 GUARANTEE

$5,000 Guarantee Gamesmanship

Let me congratulate you on your $5,000 Guarantee. . . . I had never seen that before. . . . "Here are the stocks we want you to buy and here's our guarantee that they will make money for you."

Super! I like it when people stick out their necks like that.

Of course, when someone does this, there are always sharks around to take advantage of it. I read the rules of the guarantee a few times but couldn't make up my mind as to whether the following scheme is legal.

For instance, someone buys a few shares of every new Company of the Month. And, after three years, he submits his claim for the $5,000 by submitting only those confirmation forms for the companies on which he lost money. And, he would say he accidentally only bought those stocks that didn't do so well!

If it isn't legal, then I must have missed it in the rules. If it isn't in the rules, this is a friendly warning that the sharks may be coming.

— Wim Sanders, Meldert, Belgium

We appreciate Wim's thoughtfulness in alerting us to possible "sharks.". . . In the Dec '02 edition, we said there might be a certain amount of gamesmanship.

When we announced the terms of the $5,000 Guarantee, we purposely did not fill them with legalese. But, we think we've thought this through quite thoroughly. . . . Here is how we'd react to the "scheme" Buckaroo Sanders outlined:

(1) The schemer has to follow the Bowser Game Plan, which means he has to have at least 12 different Bowser stocks by the end of the three years. Over that three-year period, there are only 36 new Companies of the Month. Based on our past record, it is not likely that a third of them are going to be bad.

(2) The applicant will have to sign a document certifying that the stocks he submits were the only Bowser equities bought in those three years. Once he signs that document, we will turn it over to counsel, who will ask the applicant to verify his/her statement. If they are not cooperative, legal action will be taken and the applicant may be spending more in legal fees than the $5,000 is worth.

More Details on the $5,000 Guarantee

I am wondering about your $5,000 guarantee. When you say that this offer only pertains to your recommendations, are you talking about the current Company of the Month? Can I buy past Companies of the Month?

— Howard M. Sears, North Uxbridge, MA

You can buy past Companies of the Month if they are still on our buy list on page 4 and if they are still $3 a share or less.

We are amused that some folks think we will pay them $5,000 if they make money on our stocks during a three-year period. We clearly state that we will pay $5,000 if you do not make money by explicitly following our Game Plan for three years.

Also, we expect that this offer will incite a certain amount of gamesmanship. For example, someone would buy one stock at the beginning of a three-year period and then 11 more just before the period is up. And, since they will have had the bulk of the portfolio for only a month or less, the stocks therein would not have had time to develop. So, he or she could claim no money was made.

We'll be on the lookout.

BOWSERIZING A PORTFOLIO

EACH JANUARY, THE *BULL & BEAR FINANCIAL REPORT* (800/336-2855) asks us for our top stock picks for the coming year. On Jan. 8, 2001, ten stocks were selected and $1,000 was theoretically invested in each one. In Portfolio One we show what would have happened if we had just held and not made any changes. In Portfolio Two, the Bowser Game Plan is used. Portfolio Three demonstrates how the Proceeds from Sales in Portfolio Two could have been utilized to create a new one—still using the $10,000 invested in January 2001.

Portfolio One

STOCK	PRICE JAN '01	NO. OF SHARES	VALUE SEPT '02
Alpha Pro (APT)	1.13	885 x	0.88 = 778.80
Allied Dev (ALDV)	3.00	333 x	0.22 = 73.26
Flour City (FCIN)	1.88	532 x	0.01 = 5.32
Emerson Radio (MSN)	1.19	840 x	3.10 = 2604.00
Exploration (TXCO)	2.88	347 x	5.38 = 1866.86
Stratesec (SFT)	2.38	420 x	0.16 = 67.20
Poore Bros (SNAK)	2.69	372 x	2.38 = 885.36
Sherwood (SHD)	2.38	420 x	5.00 = 2100.00
Rag Shops (RAGS)	2.09	478 x	4.00 = 1912.00
Magellan Pet (MPET)	1.13	885 x	0.91 = 805.35
			11,098.15

On Jan '01 $10,000 was invested—$1,000 in each stock. In 21 months there was an 11% gain; annualized 5.6%. This is the normal way of evaluating a portfolio.

We shift to Portfolio Two as we begin to demonstrate how the Bowser Plan can be implemented with this portfolio.

Portfolio Two

	VALUE 10/16/02	PROCEEDS FROM SALES
Alpha Pro	778.80	
Allied Devices	Sold Jun '02	0.52 x 333 = 173.16
Flour City	Sold May '01	3.72 x 266 = 989.52
	Sold Jul '01	2.79 x 266 = 742.14
Emerson Radio	Sold Aug '02	2.59 x 420 = 1087.80
	Sold Sep '02	2.98 x 420 = 1251.60
Exploration	Sold Apr '02	5.76 x 173 = 996.48
	Sold May '02	6.17 x 174 = 1073.58
Stratesec	Sold May '02	0.43 x 420 = 180.60
Poore Bros.	751.44	
Sherwood	Sold Sep '01	4.80 x 210 = 1008.00
	Sold Jan '02	6.07 x 210 = 1274.70
Rag Shops	Sold May '02	4.25 x 239 = 1015.75
	Sold Jun '02	4.95 x 239 = 1183.05
Magellan Pet	Sold Jul '02	0.83 x 885 = 734.55
		11,710.93

Of the $11,710.93 generated by the Proceeds from Sales, $8,000 will be expended on the purchase of eight new stocks. See Portfolio Three.

We will transfer to Portfolio Three $3,710.93 of our surplus Proceeds from Sales (11,710.93 - 8,000 = 3,710.93).

Portfolio Three

STOCK	NO. OF SHARES		PRICE 10/16/02		VALUE
Alpha Pro (APT)	885	x	0.78	=	690.30
Poore Bros (SNAK)	372	x	2.02	=	751.44
Immucell (ICCC)	444	x	1.83	=	812.52
Contango (MCF)	335	x	3.22	=	1078.70
Harvey Elec (HRVE)	781	x	0.90	=	702.90
Phoenix Gold (PGLD)	487	x	1.77	=	861.99
Nyer Medical (NYER)	500	x	1.73	=	865.00
Leading Brands (LBIX)	370	x	3.19	=	1180.30
Chad Therapeu (CTU)	386	x	2.52	=	972.72
Hi-Shear Tech (HSR)	505	x	2.60	=	1313.00
					9,228.87
			Proceeds from Sales		3,710.93
					12,939.80

When a stock was sold in Portfolio Two, a replacement issue was purchased that was the most recent Company of the Month.

Summary

✔ On our original $10,000 investment we now have a gain of 29%, for an annualized gain of 15.3%.

✔ Most important, we now have 10 stocks that can lead us to more gains.

"John, I think we'd do better investing using the Bowser Way."

FREQUENTLY ASKED QUESTIONS

When we give speeches or appear on radio, invariably certain questions are asked. Here are our answers:

Question No. 1: Aren't these little stocks illiquid? Don't you have difficulty selling them?

This is worrying about a problem that doesn't exist. . . . We have been buying and selling stocks under $3 for three decades and that hasn't been a negative, nor have our subscribers complained about liquidity.

Yes, but I once owned one of those little stocks and some days it didn't even trade.

If you owned 500,000 shares and the company had two million shares outstanding, you would have a problem disposing of them at a reasonable price. But, minipricers only buy 100, 200, 1,000 or 5,000 shares at a time.

Question No. 2: Where can I get a quote on your stocks?

They trade mostly on Nasdaq, but in the 28 years we've been publishing *The Bowser Report* we've also had stocks on the New York and American Exchanges. Quotes are available every day in *The Wall Street Journal*, *Investor's Business Daily* and some local newspapers. (*Barron's* has a complete list every weekend.) Plus, online you can get quotes any time of the day.

Question No. 3: You advocate owning 12 to 18 different microcap stocks. Doesn't it take a lot of time to follow them?

With a computer, there's nothing to it. However, even if you rely on newspapers, it still doesn't take that much time. And, if you follow the Game Plan, you'll be making money. That is a pleasant task—regardless of the time.

Question No. 4: In your Selling Plan, you say to sell half of your holdings when the stock has doubled over your purchase price, and then sell the remainder when it drops back 25% from its high after doubling. In determining the selling price, do you include commissions?

You should not include commissions. For example, if you buy at $2 and it goes to $4—sell half of your holdings at $4 or as near it as you can. Brokerage fees have been reduced to the point that they are not an important consideration in the investment picture. Plus, trying to add in the commissions is an unnecessary complication. Let's keep it as simple as we can.

Question No. 5: You say some people buy each of your Company of the Month recommendations. If they do that long enough, won't they own 60 or 70 stocks?

The question implies you never sell. But, these stocks do move up and trigger the Selling Plan. Also, not all of our picks pan out, so we suggest you sell because of their poor performance. . . . Our 2002 Investor of the Year, Joe Videmsek, buys each of our new selections. But, when we talked to him, he only owned 16, because he had sold so many during the years.

Question No. 6: Before you recommend a company, do you talk to the chief executive officer?

We share the sentiments of Robert Olstein, a mutual fund manager, who told *Forbes* (2/19/01): "Why should I talk to the ministers of propaganda? I want to see what people do, not what they say." . . . Instead, he looks at financial records, especially footnotes.

We think the term "propaganda minister" is rather harsh. However, most leaders are an optimistic bunch. I'd be shocked to hear one say, "Our company has no future and buying our stock would be a big mistake." They are masters of the spin.

However, after we have recommended a stock, we have had occasion to contact and converse with CEOs. . . . We don't want to paint a picture of ruthless exploiters. We have found many to be fine people. After all, CEOs frequently are the difference between success and failure for a company.

Question No. 7: What do you look for in a stock?

The ideal minipriced issue should have no long-term debt, two million shares or less and increasing sales and earnings for the last five years. But, it is not often we find such a wonderful creature. Consequently, we have to compromise—mostly on the number of shares outstanding. However, if the insiders own a big chunk and the float is comparatively small, that makes us happy.

Question No. 8: Why don't you use P/Es, price-to-sales ratios and some other measurement devices?

A price-to-earnings ratio and some other ratios are useful in comparing large, mature corporations. But, with these little ones, the P/Es are usually high and are not indicative of future performance.

Question No. 9: When are you going to retire?

When the moon stops shining and the sun stops rising.

*Ask Me No (Hard) Questions,
And I'll Tell You . . .*

THE R. MAX BOWSER SAGA

MR. BOWSER IS THE EDITOR/PUBLISHER OF *THE BOWSER Report*, which was started in the 1970s and is the only investment newsletter for stocks $3 a share or less. In 1990, he inaugurated *The Bowser Directory of Small Stocks*, which is a computer-generated compilation of between 700 and 800 low-priced equities.

Born in Celina, Ohio, Bowser exhibited an early interest in journalism. He was editor of his high school newspaper for three years. After high school, he worked on weekly Ohio newspapers, first in Coldwater and then in Eaton. On the *Eaton Press-Review*, he was the editor and a "string" correspondent for the Associated Press, the *Dayton Journal-Herald* and the *Cincinnati Times-Star*.

R. Max Bowser

Later he was employed on newspapers in California: Monrovia, Arcadia and in the San Fernando Valley. His newspaper career was interrupted, however, by military service. During a tour in the Air Force, he went from a headquarters clerk to an intelligence officer.

In fact, he made a career of the Air Force. He served a total of 24 years. Besides the Philippines,

Japan and Korea, he was stationed in Germany, Turkey and Vietnam, plus various state-side bases. He retired in April 1970 with the rank of lieutenant colonel.

While at his last duty station in the Air Force—Langley Air Force Base In Hampton, Virginia—Bowser became interested in the stock market. And, he decided to make it his specialty during his post-military career.

His first step in that new career was to go to college to broaden his business background. In the spring of 1973, he graduated magna cum laude from Thomas Nelson Community College in Hampton, Virginia with two associate degrees—one in accounting and one in business administration.

From 1973 to 1979, he further studied the stock market, refining his techniques for investing in low-priced equities. It was also during this period he decided to concentrate on stocks selling for $3 a share or less. Too, he then determined the format for the newsletter, principally by mailing it to a select group across the country and considering their various suggestions.

Although it initially had only 40 paid subscribers, *The Bowser Report* is now in the top 3%, circulation-wise, among the hundreds of investment newsletters.

Bowser finds his experience as a military intelligence analyst is not dissimilar to his present role as a securities analyst. The technique is the same—bringing together various facets of information and, from this mass of information, deducing future action. Also, his many years of writing simplifies his task of monthly preparing *The Bowser Report*.

COMMENTS FROM THOSE WHO HAVE USED MAX BOWSER'S INVESTMENT STRATEGIES

Max, there is a reason you have successfully published your newsletter for so many years. You do your homework, care about subscribers and thus have a savvy subscriber base.

– Dave Olson, Englewood, CO

A few weeks ago I took a subscription to your newsletter. I must say it is one of the best I have ever read.

– Wim Sanders, Meldert, Belgium

Even though I am not anywhere near a millionaire using your recommendations and plan, the entertainment value as a hobby that I have gotten out of it is priceless. I love your publication.

– Bert Kober, Bloomfield Hills, MI

Let me repeat what I have stated previously. You have the finest publication of its kind on the planet.

– William P. Delp, Kinderhook, NY

The Bowser Report is an extraordinary newsletter that fully informs its subscribers in a very truthful and trusted approach about all its recommendations.

– John Basil, Buffalo, NY

I have only been involved with stocks for two years and have provided myself with many learning opportunities in that time. Your *Bowser Report* offers a common sense plan and useful information in a format I can understand.

– Daniel Hewitt, Holts Summit, MO

Thanks for providing us with an excellent outlook on the market. It takes many hours to study and review companies. I personally think you are doing a good job. It saves me a lot of time. I rely on your advice 100%.

– Theodore S. Hudson, Madrid, Spain

My grandfather was a big fan of yours. In fact, every two weeks he would meet with his friends to discuss your stock recommendations. I like your writing and your recommendations.

– C. Mar, Seattle, WA

The Motley Fools said in the *Dayton* (Ohio) *Daily News* that no one can make money with "penny stocks" and those that sell for less than $5 per share. . . . Don't believe it, Max. I'm a follower of the Bowser Plan and believe there are lots of winners at $3 or less. Love your publication and your Plan.

– Edward J. Washington, Troy, OH

Thanks to you and your team for an honest, inexpensive and intelligent newsletter.

– Michael J. Mayrzedt, Linz, Austria

Max, keep up the good sleuthing. You can't be right 100% of the time. Your batting average looks pretty good to me.

– Roger J. Bakken, St. Paul, MN

This trip, like many of our others, is what we call a Bowser trip. Max Bowser, whom I've never met, runs a stock advisory service. He picks and follows stocks under $3. Most important, he has a Sell Plan. It is because of the results of this service that we travel so much. Max knows how to make profits. His monthly newsletter has been a consistent winner over the years.

– Warren Kaplan, Boca Raton, FL

THE HUMOROUS SIDE

"Basically it's a stock that if a chain of near-miraculous events would happen to occur, you'd make a bundle!"

My wife doesn't want me to talk to you penny stock brokers. What'd you say? An HIV cure for only 3¢ a share. Put me down for 1,000 shares.

WALL STREET'S CONCEPT OF MINIPRICED INVESTORS

Some stocks are bigger and stronger than others

INDEX

- A -
Agnew, Bose 63
Air Methods 61
Aztec Partners 61

- B -
Bakken, Roger 63, 99
Barron's 37, 48, 51, 91
Bienick, Rose Marie 63
Blinder, Meyer 55
Blinder Robinson & Co. 55
Bostrom, Chuck 63
Bowser Directory Of Small Stocks 41, 42, 95
Bowser Historical Review 49
Boyer, D. Royce 29
Brown & Co. 62
Buckaroos 12, 13, 19, 20, 69
Bull & Bear Financial Report . 85
Burke, Michael 26, 69
Business Week 48

- C -
Clear One Communications 46, 77
Clements, Jonathan 52
Comtech Telecommunications . 61
Cramer, James 33, 35

- D -
Diversification 10, 15, 19

- E -
Einstein, Albert 78
Enders, Theresa 57
Enron 47, 54, 70

- F -
Flaherty, Robert J. 10
Forbes Magazine 48, 51, 93
Forsyth, Randall W. 51

- G -
Glassman, James K. 39

- H -
Home Depot 34

- I -
I-Know-Best Approach 25, 28
Investment Company Institute . 29
Investor's Business Daily . 48, 91

- K -
Kiplinger's 48, 53

- L -
Leverage 15, 19, 58
Lynch, Peter 31

- M -
Malkiel, Burton 30, 31
Meet The Millionaire Next Door 62
Merrill Lynch 49
Microcaps 9, 19, 38, 41-43, 48, 58, 92
Minipriced Stocks 19, 20, 24, 25, 28, 41, 48, 52, 58, 59, 67, 91, 94
Money Magazine 48
Moneypaper 9, 25, 27, 69
Moneypaper Portfolio 26, 27
Monterey Pasta 60-62
Mullin, Linda 63

- N -
Nelson, Vita 25, 96

- O -
Olstein, Robert 93
One-Month-At-A-Time Deal 25, 28
One-Shot Method 25, 26

- P -
Palaslewski, Stephen J. ....
Picchietti, John 41
Proceeds From Sales .. 16, 20-24, 26, 27, 39, 59, 75, 85, 87, 88

- R -

Research 15, 28, 47, 54, 79
Rhodes, David 63
Risk 19, 20, 35, 51
Rogers, John W. 51

- S -

Sanders, Wim 81, 82
Schwab, Charles 62, 70
Sears, Howard M. 82
Selling Plan ... 16, 20, 22, 67, 77, 78, 92, 93

- T -

Templeton, John 51
Tobias, Andrew 38
Twain, Mark 68

- U -

U.S. Securities & Exchange Commission 55, 77

- V -

Vanguard Group 32
Videmsek, Joe 57-62, 64, 65, 93

- W -

Wall Street Journal 39, 48, 52, 91

- Z -

Zestos, George K. 42, 43

The Bowser Report

THE PREMIER NEWSLETTER FOR MINIPRICED STOCKS SINCE 1976

If you enjoyed reading this book and the concept outlined, you will also enjoy reading *The Bowser Report*. Highlights of this 10-page monthly newsletter are:

(1) **Company of the Month** – One stock is selected for detailed analysis.

(2) **Minipriced Stocks in Buying Range** – A list of those stocks on the NYSE, ASE and Nasdaq markets that have a Bowser Rating of 8 or more.

(3) **Follow-Through** – Past recommendations are continuously reviewed.

(4) **Feature Articles** – Feature articles are written in an informal, humorous style.

(5) **Bowser Buckaroos Speak** – In which we respond to letters from our subscribers on issues of universal interest.

ALL THIS IS AVAILABLE FOR ONE OF THE LOWEST SUBSCRIPTION PRICES AROUND!

For a sample copy of this unique newsletter, just mail in this coupon.

R. Max Bowser
The Bowser Report
P.O. Box 6278
Newport News, VA 23606

Please send to me FREE and without obligation a sample copy of *The Bowser Report*.

Name _____

Address _____

City _____ State _____ Zip _____

P.O. BOX 6278 NEWPORT NEWS, VIRGINIA 23606 (757) 877-5979

MILLIONAIRE RESOURCE LIST

The following books and audiocassettes are informative and based on tried and proven methods by the authors. You may request these products from your book dealer, or order directly from the publisher.

AUDIOCASSETTES

How To Get Rich and Stay Rich
A Live Speech by Fred J. Young   Retail Price: $9.95

This popular and humorous speech by Fred J. Young explains how this multimillionaire made his fortune by investing a portion of his salary in a few shares of stock on a regular basis. At this time, his net worth is over $3 million.

Don't Get Mad — Get Rich
A Live Speech by Fred J. Young   Retail Price: $9.95

Humorous true adventures that Fred J. Young had during his journey toward becoming a multimillionaire. Fun to listen to and full of stock market wisdom.

BOOKS

Making Dollars With Pennies:
How the Small Investor Can Beat the Wizards on Wall Street
Author: R. Max Bowser   Retail Price: $19.95

Penny Stock Winners:
True Stories of Successful Investors
Author: R. Max Bowser   Retail Price: $19.95

Guaranteed Profits:
The Only Stock Market Investment System
That Comes With A $5,000 Guarantee
Author: R. Max Bowser   Retail Price: $19.95

All the above audiocassettes and books are published by:

MARATHON INTERNATIONAL BOOK COMPANY
P.O. Box 40   Phone: (812) 273-4672
Madison, IN 47250-0040   Fax: (812) 273-8964
U.S.A.   e-mail: jwortham@seidata.com

ORDER FORM

Quantity		Unit Price	Total For Product
	AUDIOCASSETTES		
_____	*How To Get Rich and Stay Rich* A speech by Fred J. Young	$9.95	$_____
_____	*Don't Get Mad — Get Rich* A speech by Fred J. Young	$9.95	$_____
	BOOKS		
_____	*Making Dollars With Pennies: How The Small Investor Can Beat The Wizards On Wall Street* Book by R. Max Bowser	$19.95	$_____
_____	*Penny Stock Winners: True Stories of Successful Investors* Book by R. Max Bowser	$19.95	$_____
_____	*Guaranteed Profits: The Only Stock Market Investment System That Comes With A $5,000 Guarantee* Book by R. Max Bowser	$19.95	$_____

POSTAGE

Regular Mail: $2 for first book or audiocassette, $1 for each additional.
Priority Mail: $4 for first book or audiocassette, $1 for each additional.
Foreign Orders (Air Mail): $4 for first book or audiocassette, $2 for each additional.

Total Amount for Products Ordered: $_____

Total Amount for Shipping: $_____

Grand Total Amount: $_____

Name _____

Address _____

City _____ State _____ Zip _____

Send order form and payment in U.S. funds to:

MARATHON INTERNATIONAL BOOK COMPANY
P.O. Box 40
Madison, IN 47250-0040
U.S.A.

ORDER FORM

Quantity		Unit Price	Total For Product
	AUDIOCASSETTES		
_____	*How To Get Rich and Stay Rich* A speech by Fred J. Young	$9.95	$_____
_____	*Don't Get Mad — Get Rich* A speech by Fred J. Young	$9.95	$_____
	BOOKS		
_____	*Making Dollars With Pennies: How The Small Investor Can Beat The Wizards On Wall Street* Book by R. Max Bowser	$19.95	$_____
_____	*Penny Stock Winners: True Stories of Successful Investors* Book by R. Max Bowser	$19.95	$_____
_____	*Guaranteed Profits: The Only Stock Market Investment System That Comes With A $5,000 Guarantee* Book by R. Max Bowser	$19.95	$_____

POSTAGE

Regular Mail: $2 for first book or audiocassette, $1 for each additional.
Priority Mail: $4 for first book or audiocassette, $1 for each additional.
Foreign Orders (Air Mail): $4 for first book or audiocassette, $2 for each additional.

Total Amount for Products Ordered: $_____

Total Amount for Shipping: $_____

Grand Total Amount: $_____

Name _____

Address _____

City _____ State _____ Zip _____

Send order form and payment in U.S. funds to:

MARATHON INTERNATIONAL BOOK COMPANY
P.O. Box 40
Madison, IN 47250-0040
U.S.A.

Printed in the United States
44537LVS00004B/1-9